Garden of different flowers

Shilpa Suresh

BookLeaf Publishing
India | USA | UK

Presentation by *BookLeaf Publishing*

Web: www.bookleafpub.com

E-mail: info@bookleafpub.com

ISBN: 9789357447874

First edition 2022

DEDICATION

This book is dedicated to my mother.

Mommy, If you were right beside me and not so far away,

Things would have been simpler and I could have just told you all I wanted to say.

But don't worry now it's all for you written and saved away.

But this time I thought I'll just spice things up in a poetic way!

ACKNOWLEDGEMENT

Firstly, I feel grateful to have had a dear friend who encouraged and supported me. I thank him for taking the time to read through my poems and even going as far as to ask the reason behind why I wrote each one and what every sentence I wrote actually meant. I felt heard and recognized which made me feel happy and excited while writing the ones on this book.

Secondly, I acknowledge 'Bookleaf publications' whose 21 day writing challenge came right at the time when I was on holidays and needed that push to write.

Lastly but in no way the least, I would like to heartily thank my parents. Who, whatever happens and whatever I choose to do, always stand with me, supporting me in every way. They are like pen and paper to my thoughts if that would describe it.

PREFACE

Every day you get up feeling different,
Every day you are a different version.
And that's okay.

Because sometimes it's cold,
Sometimes it's sunny,
Sometimes it rains,
Sometimes it snows.

When the weather herself changes everyday,
Why not let all the different flowers in your
garden stay :)

CONTENTS

Worthwhile

When the setting sun baths thy room in Amber
glow,
Sitting at thy desk, lazily stretching thy feet,
Silence engulfs thee,
Mind isn't controlled, it's left free.

Racing thoughts, not one do pass,
In thy consciousness, nothing's trapped,
Loosen thyself,
The leashes that were holding on to thee.

Pity those with too much to do,
Ye' mind's processing through,
Great journeys ye'll gone through,
Whatever time it needs's worthwhile too.

Haircut!

I have plaited, tied, and left them loose,
My long strands of hair in good profuse,
Well I hoped they would grow until my shoes,
Then as Rapunzel can I be introduced.

A walk, a run, a play, a fight,
The next day in broad daylight,
What I thought yesterday night,
Doesn't suit my mood quite that right.

Hmmm long hair takes time to grow,
I tell my momy about it so,
A fast change shouldn't be this slow,
To the parlor is where I want to go! '

Sitting now comfortably on the seat,
At the man who'll cut down my hair neat,
Pinpointing on that hairstyle sheet,
A Diana cut! I grin all sweet.

The hesitant man now takes a glance,
At the side where my momy stands,
Seeing my momy in an assuring stance,
The man now in a mild trance,

But slowly does he get used to it,
Chop, chop, chop he cuts at it,
My hair's all around where I sit,
I relax until he is finished with it.

When all is done well I do look deep,
At myself in the mirror from hair to feet,
Not knowing accepting this would be this steep,
Now I look at myself like a new person I meet!

Sonnet I

What we know of us, do they not,
In waning hope on themselves, which do they
pin on us,
With needles of all sizes they don't know how to
sort,
Mixing them all up making it worser that 'twas.
Needles of advice we don't ask for,
What you need to stich on yourself,
Ye' end up picking on us for,
 Wherefore hast thou lost yourself.
Dripping with drops of blood,
Our soul's smeared with your lost cause,
Ye'll poisoning us at the bud,
Nay ye'll don't even oft know when to pause.
Your broken needles keep them to you,
We don't need any of 'em on us to sew.

Dream will I of great things

Dream will I of great things,
As free as the bird sings,
As free as the wind blows,
Dream will I of great things.

Why would I trap my dreams into webs,
Of reality and the doubt on myself,
When my mind would like to heed no ear,
To thoughts that want to pull it near,
To simple and heard of things,
Things that with it brings,
Measurable success all caught on strings,
By others designed to chart my path,
To be exactly as theirs from the start,
Which will lead me to nowhere though,
Next to where they stand but one step low.

So dream will I of great things,
Things that with it brings,
A joy so profound,
That my heart sings,
So dream will I of great things.

Reflection in the mirror- A tragic love story

The curtains on the stage pull apart,
To reveal a man with his hand on his heart;
Leaning down on the wooden floor,
He is seen confessing his love to her.

The audience all leaning now,
Because in front of the man is only a mirror
somehow.
Aaah he's shown practicing maybe,
But the mirror is at 45 degrees they see.

That mirror is actually reflecting someone
behind,
She is behind the stage, not in sight.
That beautiful young women's reflection's on
the mirror,
Oh so that handsome smart lad is proposing to
her.

A split second and the curtain drops,
Whatever needed to be shown is shown enough,
That women's voice is heard in the room,
A loud furious scream follows shocking the
audience anew.

"When I stand independently,
They look at me demeaningly.

When I play up my feminity,
They make me feel like I'm just good looks and
puppetry.

Accepting that okay maybe that's how life is,
I stand next to the man I love longingly.

He loves me too,
I had told my self self-assuringly.
But there look!
That witless love of mine stands there as if
mocking me,

Proposing to my reflection

If that's what he needs,
And that's all he sees,
Oh well common you Nincompoop!
I am way more than just my reflection in that
mirror you see! "

When the wind
blows at me

When the wind blows at me,
The chill cold breeze where I stand,
Loosing all sense of warmth, Shivering,
My thoughts racing, as if searching for heat.

I bend in, inside of me,
A void I see, with no company,
Love was lost and was never again found.
The chill breeze, breaths down on me.

People clothed in fur and boots,
They seem to be mindful of where they are,
Or what they feel,
I seem to have lost my senses,

Some sense that drowned in that void in me.

With my glass slippers

Once when I wanted to try something new,
I picked an adventure sport to do,
A tandem Skydive over the Palm Jumeira in
Dubai,
Imagining my brave self proudly waving
goodbye.

One month was quite a nice time,
For me to imagine what I was not for sometime.
But with my jumping date approaching quick,
Oh my imaginary brave self mockingly gives a
wink .

People say distance blurs out the reality ,
Ha well back then I seemed to have had a
different mentality.
Don't people say we need to step out of our
comfort zone!
Oh well doing that would I though like to break
a bone?

Too many thoughts going in my head,
I can't change what lies ahead.
Maybe I don't really need to step out of my
comfort zone you know,
When I know exactly what I'm going to
undergo?

So I watch Skydiving videos on repeat,
In an attempt to make my fear obsolete,
I listen to them talking about how they feel,
Slowly I built for myself in the process a
concrete zeal.

Now with so many times vividly imagining it in
my head,
What is to be expected is in my mind now fed,
What was then unknown with uncertainty,
My oozing fear is now measurable in quantity !

Oh so from my comfort zone why would I ever
part,
When I can rather extend it and conquer all that
was apart,
So that with my glass slippers I can chart,
Territories that weren't mine from the start?

Behind those closed doors

One fine day when I had nothing left to do,
I tried to open those doors that had been shut for
years,
I found myself looking at all the beautiful things
I possess,
Until all forgotten memories slowly had me
possessed.

One by one my neatly kept souvenirs,
Looked at me longingly,
Until I reached my hands and lifted them up,
Did I not know how much dust had been built
up.

My favourite dress I had saved for special
occasions,
With all its glitter and shimmering stones,
Neatly still hangs on that side door,
Doesn't though fit me anymore.

That delicate watch once gifted to me,
Too delicate to be used so sat right there all
along,
I had done my best to immortalize it,
But no more can I see the time with it.

There is this lipstick I had once bought,
To be used only when I want to feel special,
Looking at its expiry date,
Slowly with guilt did it make me inundate.

But the small purse with all the money I saved,
Neatly stored to be used only when it is needed,
I'll take at least that with me now and place it on
my bed,
As company on my death bed.

As free as my free verse

The sun shining through the curtains,
Wakes me up from my deep slumber.
Rubbing my eyes and yawning loud,
What a cozy day to wake up to .

Lying in bed I take note of how I feel;
My body feels relaxed and calm,
My mind is clear to start the day afresh,
With no trace of yesterdays exertion to be found.

Looking around my beautiful pastel room,
Decorated with love,
I feel a sense of security,
A bliss, an affirmative that nothing can ever go
wrong.

Sitting in bed I pick up my planner,
 Neatly placed on my bed side table,
An exciting day to be alive!
Lot of things to look forwards to today.

So with a nod of my head, I acknowledge my
existence,
With a smile, I affirm that I'm on the right track,
With sitting up straight and tall, I allow myself
to breath into the fresh air,
With a pleasant humm, I know I feel alive.

~Whenever I get out of bed, I revive.
Negatives of yesterday do not survive.
I'm a blooming flower and I always thrive. ~

[You might wonder why this poem doesn't quite
seem to rhyme,
But hey there is a name to it!
Free verse is what I'm writing this time :)]

The sucking machine

Imagine there is this mystery,
When you close your eyes there is a strong
force,
It sucks you in into a swirling wind,
Where you don't know what's happening around
you anymore.

You realize the world is now big,
Bigger than you,
You have shrunk,
As small as you can go,
You shrunk,
All far too low,
The world is compared to you,
An undecipherable alien view.

Tall tall creatures,
Tall and high,
Big big mouths,
As big as their lie,
Panting young, heroic lads,
Running like hamsters placed in labs,

A weird scene from your vision,
Is something not you imagined,
That silly thing that sucked you in,
Into something you didn't want to be in,
Just wanted to show you what you have actually
been in.

A made goose race of some serious sort,
Where you see what everyone's upto at each
spot,
You know not why or how you got in there,
But all you see is that everyone along with you
is right there.

Your pointless race,
Not knowing what you chase,
We need to cover your windows with curtains,
To block out this case,
Of unhuman things we have started to do,
Which would one day pull our brains right in to,
Some sucking machine like the one you're in,
To shrink everything up and throw it in,
Some big open space for a bin.

Ring-Ring-Ring goes my alarm clock

Ring, ring, ring my alarm clock sings,
Every morning at the dawn of day,
My bright yellow clock never does forget to
ring,
Even when I threaten to throw her away.

When I am busy dreaming of vacationing,
In some peaceful Island far away,
She screams at me with a sound so annoying,
That immediately shuts down the picture on my
minds display.

Yes sometimes I do feel bad,
To never leave my bed when she rings,
But more than that what's really sad,
Is that with anger her I fling.

I've thrown her right at the floor,
I've muffled her right into the sheets,
But all along until I'm sore,
She never stops her singing beats.

One fine day though I think she will stop,
Trying in vain to wake me up,
That fine day I will plop,
In my bed all day until I drop!
(Pls. .. I mean until my bed gets tired of holding
me in,
So she pushes me out into the dustbin :/
Yaikees :0)

Ode to my dwelling

What have I got, when the rain pours down,
Shelter's never found, when I go looking for
one.
When the Sun though shines bright, with a
radiant warmth,
Shelter right on my side, is always found.
My life you see, is an Irony.

What hast the Gods planned for me?
I know not much, about those mysterious
shelters,
But I do know that they are like petals on a
flower.
The one on the same bouquet,
Not in mine, but the neighbor right next to me.

I shant look beyond.
What hast thou not given to me?
Thou sacred, safe heavenly glow,
With all thy locked chambers, just for me.
Partitions, to keep me,
Partitions thou hast made ,to suit my every
journey.

I'll move through life in thee,
For every segment of life, you have a new home
for me.

I'll move through life in thee,
For every experience you'll keep it locked for
me.

I'll move through life in thee,
As for I can open a new partition when one's
slippery.

I'll move through life in thee,
As all my burdens you'll carry for me.

I'll move through life in thee,
So that with every step I move higher with ease,
The last steps baggage will never be found in
me.

I'll move through life in thee,
With a comfortable assurity,
That always my dwelling I have with me.

What do I loose with tears I shed in time

What do I loose with tears I shed in time,
When light as a feather I feel each time.

Who art though ye to question me,
When what's right and what's wrong is unclear.

Have I lost the freedom to grieve,
When I get conscious of what you perceive.

Whence can I though fill my half broken soul,
Let me at least pour what's not mine anymore.

Scream is a shout a shrill unpleasant tone,
Cry on the other hand a rather silent mourn.

Would ye be as kind and allow a person be,
Free with his emotions and true to thyself.

Do we need to ask permission time and again,
To allow energy to flow and not just stagnate in
pain ?

Ms. Bright pink &
Mr. Stylish red

Once when I was walking down a road,
Was when I saw a big green toad,
She hopped and jumped right in front of me,
So I bent down to clearly see.

Her eyes were so big and cute,
She also wore a bright pink suit,
Her hair was curly, free and loose,
Which ran down until her shoes.

Now right behind me where I stood,
Something moved so I turned to look,
Well behind the grass now I could see,
Something was certainly hiding from me!

A small red shoe on one foot,
Perfectly matching its stylish suit,
Peek-a-boo another toad is here,
Hiding so, oh-so-near!

That's when I realize that Ms. Bright pink
seemed to be,
Jumping and hopping around in victory,
Poor Mr. Stylish red next time needs to sneak,
Better to win at Hide-and-Seek!

That silly garbage truck

What is that sound I hear,
Like a scream, a roar, a zoo is near,
When I am fast asleep tucked into the sheets,
That silly garbage truck is here.

Early in the morning before the sun,
That dreadful noise I try to shun,
I have already tried blocking it with a bun,
But an eatable stuffed in my ear's no fun.

On summer days when my room is hot,
I don't shut my windows till they lock,
There comes that fainting smell like from in a
pot,
Where some dead mice has been left to rot.

So early morning I lift my sleepy head,
Right up from those soft pillows on my bed,
Because of all the nasty things with which my
ears and nose are fed,
My poor pale skin matches a bright tomato red.

Elegy to a once blooming ally

Yet once more in solemn grief,
Thou hast truculently our branches snapped.
What could have become an impregnable root,
Lies now uprooted at the found.

Those tender stems vigilantly grown,
That sapling nurtured punctilious,
By mine and yours our delightful heed,
Now rot with pests of our doubts entrapped.

Those ghosts of doom meander,
Our efficacious perceptions supplant.
Exuberant charms fallen into frit,
Our bracing bark's girdled.

A little parched are now all other blossoming
sprouts,
Like a sorrowful undertone to every salubrious
ally,
Our cessation stands as hapless obelisk,
On my ever sceptic, blatantly waning sally.

Sonnet II

There are a million voices in my head,
Saying hundred things I always dread,
Accompanied by a hundred not said,
Phrases that would want me dead.
Because peace and quiet is never found,
Your assumptions of me get me drowned ,
And with that wisdom you possess so profound,
You walk with that imaginary crown around.
Well what joy does it bring to get along,
With people who think you are always wrong,
When I can sit alone singing a high pithed song,
Knowing clear well that I do not belong.
But still I look longingly at you from far away,
Knowing clear well that I do not want to stay.

To somewhere far away

That feeling when I lay in bed,
The day accomplished well ahead,
Of time.

Relaxing music playing in the background,
And twinkling serial lights decorating my
foreground,
This time.

Dreaming of all the good things,
Thinking of what all that joy brings,
To me.

Pleased with the world and where I'm at,
The calmness of the garden I sat,
In today.

Washes my body with a sense of relaxation,
Like the feeling after a meditation,
I get.

The long long list of tasks made today,
Lies accomplished without any delay,
This night.

But everything came along together perfectly
well,
Every task was done in success I could tell,
Today.

I don't seem to care about what time it is now,
Or if it is too late in the night to allow,
Such thoughts.

Drifting away slowly and slowly more,
My mind and body slowly make me soar,
To somewhere far away.

Moon or the sun?
Yaikees :)

Every day the sun is up,
Each time it shows up,
Every day, every time, no matter what.

But not every day the moon is up,
Sometimes only half of her shows up,
Every day, every week, she's different.

Do I be like the sun,
Always consistent and fun,
Or do I be like the moon,
Not blooming full too soon.
I know not which one to choose,
I know not how things are supposed to move.
Would you be so kind to tell me,
What I am supposed to do?

Tell me, Is it okay to take my time when I don't
feel fine,
Is it okay to be lost sometimes.
Is it okay to wander on some open fields,
Is it okay to just be there to see what it yields.

Is it okay to be the moon, all concealed,
When the sun is the one that shines so bright,
fully revealed?

Epilogue
Moon-
Excuse me?
Are you telling me that you don't see,
That even though I don't show myself full each
time,
I am consistent with what I am,
I repeat myself like a program.
I don't show up every time,
Because see I am taking the time to make myself
rhyme!
See I like to show myself some love,
And not just leave that all behind,
Because you just want me showing up.
C'mon that's too monotonous for a Moon
y'know ;)!
Shish, comparing me with the sun,
You dumbo .

In the meanwhile, me-
Yaikeeeeeee……..eeeees!
(……Need to run before Ms. Moon gets all full
and gives me her full glow)

Queen

Queen, Queen, Queen, Queen,
Yes I will make a scene,
My mind is all clear and clean,
No there is no in-between.

My castle is what I've build for me,
If you want to take a tour to see,
You won't be allowed inside for free,
You'll need to get in with a fee.

Queen,Queen,Queen, Queen,
Yes I will make a scene,
You might think I am mean,
But Royal blood is in my gene.

If you try to act like prince to me,
Then you can come, sip some tea,
But with me, when you try to disagree,
I will sting at you like a bee.

Queen, Queen, Queen, Queen,
Yes I will make a scene,
You can rent my submarine,
I'll drive for you like it's so routine,

Queen,Queen,Queen, Queen,
Yes I will make a scene,
Because why should I get stuck in-between,
When in every scene I would like to be seen.

Queen,Queen,Queen, Queen,
Yes I will make a scene,
Don't you dare try to intervene,
'Cos then it's time for Halloween!

Before I get to you

When I stand on that open field,
Facing the sun.

My vulnerability fully revealed,
To you.

I ask the green canopy to shield,
Me tight.

From the wind that's heading,
Towards me.

From that wind that's heading,
Towards me,
That would wheel me to you.
Let me love myself first,
Before I can get to you.